# What Shall I Say?

## Discerning God's Call to Ministry

A resource from the Division for Ministry
The Evangelical Lutheran Church in America

**WRITERS:**    Walter R. Bouman
Sue M. Setzer

**EDITORS:**    Madelyn H. Busse
A. Craig Settlage
Jill Carroll Lafferty
Carol L. Schickel

**COVER DESIGNER:**    Craig Claeys

| First Printing | September, 1994 |
| Second Printing | July, 1995 |
| Third Printing | July, 1998 |
| Fourth Printing | May, 1999 |
| Fifth Printing | November, 2000 |
| Sixth Printing | April, 2003 |

Bouman, Walter R.
Setzer, Sue M.
    What Shall I Say?/Walter R. Bouman, Sue M. Setzer
    ISBN 0-9636630-1-1
    AFP 34-1-2106

# Contents

Lord God,
you have called your servants
to ventures of which we cannot see the ending,
by paths as yet untrodden,
through perils unknown.
Give us faith to go out with good courage,
not knowing where we go,
but only that your hand is leading us
and your love supporting us;
through Jesus Christ our Lord. Amen

Lutheran Book of Worship, Morning Prayer

# Invitation to Discernment

*T*he question is not, "Do I have gifts for ministry?" The question is, "What gifts do I have, and for which ministry are they best suited?" This resource invites you into a process to discover your gifts and to discern the ministry to which God calls you. Discernment is perceiving the will and way of God in the church and in your life. There are no easy steps on the venture to which you are called, but the church into which you were baptized is ready to assist and support you as you search. Discernment involves prayer, personal reflection, and conversation with others, for the call is always communal, not an individual response.

You may be a college student considering several options for your baptismal call or vocation. Perhaps you sense that God may be calling you to ordained ministry or to a rostered lay ministry in the Evangelical Lutheran Church in America. You may be well into another career, but people in your congregation keep telling you they think you need to consider attending seminary for a year. *What Shall I Say?* is a challenging resource intended to state a Lutheran understanding of call and ministry, and to introduce you to the variety of ministries in the Evangelical Lutheran Church in America.

Some steps are suggested to make this resource more valuable to you: (1) write your reflections as you read this resource, (2) talk with your pastor, campus minister, a diaconal minister, deaconess, or associate in ministry about your questions and concerns, (3) underline sections of this resource that you consider especially important and write question marks and comments in the margins, (4) keep notes or a journal of your general reactions and your responses to the reflection questions to use for discussion with others. Take your time. Discerning God's will is a life-long process.

The introductory prayer sets the tone for the resource: "Lord, you have called your servants. . . ." God calls all the baptized to walk into the future for ventures unseen with the promise of God's guidance and loving support. The church needs visionary leadership for mission, and God provides the church with such leaders. This resource can help you discern whether or not you may be one of these leaders or if God is calling you to Christian ministry in daily life.

First, the gospel is proclaimed in Chapter 1, "Jesus Is Risen!" All ministry extends from the ministry of the risen Christ. "Varieties of Gifts—Varieties of Service," Chapter 2, clarifies the nature of ministry and the call of every baptized person. The Evangelical Lutheran Church in America recognizes two official or "rostered" ministries: ordained ministers (pastors and bishops) and rostered laypersons (diaconal ministers, deaconesses, and associates in ministry).

Chapter 3, "Discerning God's Call and God's Gifts," examines the discernment process and the meaning of call to ministry. "Paths to Discernment," Chapter 4, indicates directions to pursue: pray, study, and worship; talk with people who know you; seek pastoral and spiritual guidance; explore work in the church and in other occupations; and respond to God's call in faith and obedience.

"What to Expect," Chapter 5, is written for those who think they might be called to rostered ministry in this church. This chapter explains the candidacy process, the education needed for rostered ministries, the costs involved, and the church's expectation that rostered leaders will be willing to serve where the church needs them.

Chapter 6, "Power for the Challenge," concludes the work with a statement of the church's need for visionary leaders and the assurance that God provides that which is needed to respond to the call to ministry. A bibliography of selected resources lists but a few of the helpful materials available.

What you are invited to explore in this resource is nothing less than your place in the great adventure that is the Christian faith and life. It is "something grand, something all-encompassing, something necessary, vital, urgent, life giving, eternal." Now we invite you to begin the process of discernment.

This Jesus God raised up,
and of that all of us are
witnesses.

*Acts 2:32*

# CHAPTER 1

# *Jesus Is Risen!*

*T*he first disciples of Jesus were faced with an immediate need to make decisions about their calling. The most dramatic and important event in human history happened to them. Within weeks they were in Jerusalem struggling with the freedom and rejoicing in the call to be witnesses of Jesus' resurrection. It grasped and shaped them forever.

Most of those earliest Christians continued to live and work where they had been before experiencing the gospel of the risen Christ. Some discerned that they were called to give leadership to that tiny group of Jews that eventually became the global church. What all of them had in common was this one thing: In community and as individuals they were witnesses to Jesus' resurrection, and that single event would call them to a new and radically changed life.

The Christian gospel is both simple and spectacular. "Jesus is risen!" "Death no longer has dominion over him" (Romans 6:9). This is "gospel" because the word "gospel" means "good news." Both "good" and "news" are important words.

The resurrection of Jesus is the one event that continues to be news, even after many centuries. Most news is no longer news within a day, and all news stops being news in a very short time. Yet Jesus' resurrection continues to be news because it is an event that is unique in the world's history. Jesus alone has conquered death.

The resurrection of Jesus continues to be *good* news because it changes everything for us and for the world. The resurrection of Jesus is not resuscitation, a dead person being recalled to life and picking up where he or she had left off. Rather, the resurrection of Jesus proclaims him as the

Messiah of Israel and the world. It announces that the reign of God has begun and will finally be victorious. Jesus is "the first fruits of those who have died" (1 Corinthians 15:20). Therefore St. Paul gives thanks to God "who gives us the victory through our Lord Jesus Christ" (1 Corinthians 15:57). The one great liberating theme of the New Testament is that Jesus' resurrection is not so much a personal "happy ending" for Jesus himself, but that it creates or begins a salvation into which all of creation enters, in which all of humanity shares. Many examples of how this gets said by Christians could be recounted. Consider just one: On April 8, 1945, as German theologian Dietrich Bonhoeffer was being taken away by the Gestapo to his hasty trial and execution, his final words to British pilot Payne Best, his friend and fellow prisoner, were: "This is the end, but for me the beginning of life." He died early the next morning in utter confidence that death and its powers did not have the last word.

The resurrection of Jesus was and is the starting point for Christianity, for its faith and witness, for its mission and calling. The first proclamation of the disciples of Jesus was not that Jesus died for the sins of the world, although that is true, but the dramatic announcement: "This Jesus God raised up, and of that all of us are witnesses" (Acts 2:32). The resurrection is the reason *why* we pay attention to Jesus at all and it determines *how* we pay attention to Jesus. We pay attention to Jesus' life and death because he has been raised from death (why); and we confess that Jesus' life and death have ultimate and decisive importance for us (how).

Thus the resurrection of Jesus has always been and always will be the basis for everything Christian. It is the basis for the Christian church. It is the basis for Christian witness. It is the basis for our being Christian. It is the basis for all ministries of Christians, for the ministries of all

Christians in their life and work, for the ministries of those Christians who are called to ordained and rostered lay ministries within the church.

## THE NEW TESTAMENT WITNESS
## TO THE RESURRECTION

The writings of the New Testament are driven by one thing: all of them bear witness to the resurrection of Jesus. There are four key elements in that witness, and they build toward telling us what kind of event the resurrection of Jesus was and is.

First, the tomb in which Jesus was buried was empty. The Jesus who was encountered beyond death was the same Jesus who had been crucified, killed, and buried. We seek to remember loved and honored persons by preserving their places or possessions, like the home of George Washington or our grandmother's prayer book. This is our only access to someone who has died. But there is absolutely no evidence that Jesus' disciples paid attention to places or possessions associated with Jesus. They had no need for this because they were witnesses to a Lord who was beyond death!

Second, the first witnesses of the empty tomb and the risen Jesus were *women*. This does not strike us as remarkable until we remember that the testimony of women was not considered important or decisive in the ancient world. St. Paul does not even mention women in the first list of witnesses, 1 Corinthians 15:5-8. But all the Gospels, written after St. Paul's death, mention women as the initial witnesses. The cultural acceptance of their testimony had not changed when Mark's or Luke's Gospel was written. But the evangelists could not tell the story truthfully without mentioning this potentially damaging aspect. It is one of God's wonderful ironies that the credibility of the witness is strengthened today because the original witnesses lacked credibility in their culture.

Third, the disciples encountered Jesus against their expectations. They had not planned or hoped to see him again. They were filled with terror and indescribable awe. They needed to be reassured and comforted when they were encountered by him. They even needed to be taught the significance of what they were experiencing (Luke 24:25-27).

Fourth, Jesus disappeared and yet remained! The disappearances were strange, as strange as the appearances. For in disappearing, Jesus did not leave them. After the last of the disappearances, the disciples did not mourn his departure. They "returned to Jerusalem with great joy" (Luke 24:52). The meaning of the strange story of the ascension (Luke 24:50-53 and Acts 1:1-11) is indicated by Jesus' final words in the Gospel of Matthew: "I am with you always, to the end of the age" (Matthew 28:20). Jesus is no longer locked into one time and one place. Jesus "ascended" into the future, and he was therefore not gone. He was with them as the power of the future. In that power we see not only the meaning of Jesus' resurrection, but we see the full meaning of our faith and our calling to be Christians.

## THE RESURRECTION AND THE FUTURE

The disciples were encountered by Jesus as forever beyond death. They had to re-vision the future in a radical way. Stephen Hawking, one of the great theoretical experts on the meaning of time, thinks that the universe is heading toward what he calls "the big crunch," when time will collapse upon itself. Death will have the last word. For everything and everyone. If that is true, and every death seems to confirm it, then death has final power, and sin has power because of death. If we believe this, we will live aggressively, protectively, no matter who else or what else pays the cost for our surviving as long as possible. If we believe this, then we are victims of aggression and self-protection, and we will despair of liberation.

But if Jesus has the last word, then God has opened to us an eternal future in which the bond of unbreakable love cannot be overcome by death.

> *There is therefore now no condemnation for those who are in Christ Jesus. For the law of the Spirit of life in Christ Jesus has set you free from the law of sin and of death. . . . For I am convinced that neither death, nor life, nor angels, nor rulers, nor things present, nor things to come, nor power, nor height, nor depth, nor anything else in all creation, will be able to separate us from the love of God in Christ Jesus our Lord.*
>
> Romans 8:1-2, 38-39

Because Jesus has the last word, there is more to do with our lives than to preserve them. We are free from that power of death and sin that causes the world to oppress and abuse and enslave and destroy. We are free instead to offer ourselves for one another and for the world. We are set free from oppression and abuse and slavery and destruction. The final judgment upon us will not be condemnation. Jesus is the judge. Therefore we do not have to try to justify ourselves, or despair of the justification of our lives. For it was Jesus who "was raised for our justification" (Romans 4:25).

This is the meaning and basis of the church's confession that Jesus is "God from God, Light from Light, true God from true God." For as Martin Luther wrote, "god" means "that to which we look for all good." "God" means whoever or whatever has the power of the future. Because Jesus has the power of the future, we can confess him as

God and joyfully entrust ourselves, our future, and our world to him. Life, not death, will triumph. The reign of God, not the reign of death, will ultimately be victorious.

## THE RESURRECTION AND THE PAST

The disciples of Jesus confessed Jesus as God almost from the very beginning of their witness. St. Paul described Jesus as being "in the form of God" in an early hymn (Philippians 2:6). "He is the image of the invisible God. . . . He is before all things, and in him all things hold together. . . . In him all the fullness of God was pleased to dwell" (Colossians 1:15-19).

The disciples could say these astonishing things because they had reappropriated Jesus' past. Now they understood what had really been going on in Jesus' life and in Jesus' death. They remembered Jesus with altogether new eyes. When Jesus suffered, God was suffering. When Jesus died, death was happening to God. Jesus was and is the Messiah not in spite of having been crucified but as the crucified one. He "was handed over to death for our trespasses" (Romans 4:25). The good news is also "that Christ died for our sins according to the scriptures" (1 Corinthians 15:3).

Because death does not have the last word, we are free for ministry to the world.

> *For the love of Christ urges us on, because we are convinced that one has died for all; therefore all have died. And he died for all, so that those who live might live no longer for themselves, but for him who died and was raised for them.*
>
> 2 Corinthians 5:14-15

By our baptism into Christ the power of death and sin is put to death and we are free to live "by faith in the Son of God, who loved me and gave himself for me" (Galatians 2:20).

## THE MINISTRIES OF THE CHURCH

Jesus' cross and resurrection together are the basis for all ministries. The church as community and all of us as individual Christians are the new creation of the Holy Spirit. The Holy Spirit is the "down payment" on the victorious future of Christ (Ephesians 1:13-14). To have the Holy Spirit means that we are not dominated by the still-present power of death and sin in our lives and in our world. The victory belongs to Christ, and we are free to live by faith in that victory, believing, like Abraham, in the promise of the God "who gives life to the dead and calls into existence the things that do not exist" (Romans 4:17).

We are all called to be witnesses to the new life in Christ—in our lives and work, in our rest and recreation, in our homes and families, in our politics and policies.

> *So if anyone is in Christ, there is a new creation: everything old has passed away; see, everything has become new! All this is from God, who reconciled us to himself through Christ, and has given us the ministry of reconciliation; that is, in Christ God was reconciling the world to himself, not counting their trespasses against them, and entrusting the message of reconciliation to us. So we are ambassadors for Christ, since God is making his appeal through us; we entreat you on behalf of Christ, be reconciled to God. For our sake he made him to be sin who knew no sin, so that in him we might become the righteousness of God.*
>
> 2 Corinthians 5:17-21

We are still ambassadors, joyfully called to witness that Jesus is risen, that he is Messiah, that the reign of God has come and will one day be consummated, that the world is reconciled to God, that life and not death will have the last word.

The tiny community of Jesus' original disciples has become a global church. It does many things: it serves and cares; it evangelizes and baptizes; it rejoices with those who rejoice and weeps with those who weep; it worships and prays; it praises and laments; it marries and buries; it gives itself into everything that works for justice and peace. But all of these things that it does must in the end serve the one thing it is called to do: *Witness* that Jesus, the crucified one, is risen; that death no longer has dominion over him; that he alone is Lord and judge of history; that he and no other is in charge of the world's final outcome.

The church is called to be the bearer of a vision, the carrier of witness to the world's only authentic hope. It is "that society destined to be universal" (Robert Jenson).

> *The church knows what the world does not, that there is a Risen One; hopes for what the world dares not hope, that justice and love triumph; and loves what the world hates, God's will.*[1]

Listen to the author of the New Testament letter to the Christians of the ancient city of Ephesus:

> *I pray that the God of our Lord Jesus Christ, the Father of glory, may give you a spirit of wisdom and revelation as you come to know him, so that, with the eyes of your heart enlightened, you may know what is the hope to which he has called you, what are the riches of his glorious inheritance among the saints, and what is the immeasurable greatness of his power for us who believe, according to the working of his great power. God put this power to work in Christ when he raised him from the dead and seated him at his right hand in the heavenly places, far above all rule and authority and power and*

*dominion, and above every name that is named, not only in this age but also in the age to come. And he has put all things under his feet and has made him the head over all things for the church, which is his body, the fullness of him who fills all in all.*

Ephesians 1:17-23

The church that is called to be the carrier of and witness to that audacious vision is today experiencing profound challenges. These challenges affect virtually all Christians in their places of ministry and witness. The Evangelical Lutheran Church in America, empowered by the Holy Spirit, has a particular need for pastors, associates in ministry, deaconesses, and diaconal ministers who can be faithful leaders for mission. This resource asks you to think of yourself as giving this church that special kind of visionary leadership.

And what a vision! Because Jesus is risen he is the Lord of history *for the sake of the church!* His ultimate victory cannot be defeated. The church is called to participate in that victory, to be witness to that victory. The saints of God pray for the gift of visionary leaders in the church, and God does not disappoint!

*This is the feast of victory for our God. Alleluia.*

*Worthy is Christ, the Lamb who was slain,*
*whose blood set us free to be people of God.*
*Power and riches and wisdom and strength,*
*and honor and blessing and glory are his.*

*Sing with all the people of God*
*and join in the hymn of all creation:*
*Blessing and honor and glory and might*
*be to God and the Lamb forever. Amen.*

*This is the feast of victory for our God,*
*for the Lamb who was slain has begun his reign.*
*Alleluia.*

*Lutheran Book of Worship*, Holy Communion "Hymn of Praise"

*Now there are varieties of gifts, but the same
Spirit; and there are varieties of services,
but the same Lord; and there are varieties of
activities, but it is the same God who activates
all of them in everyone. To each is given the
manifestation of the Spirit for the common good.*

1 Corinthians 12:4–7

# CHAPTER 2

# *Varieties of Gifts*
# *Varieties of Service*

*C*hrist is risen!" announces the pastor on Easter Day. "Christ is risen indeed!" exclaims the community. This good news is the grounding for all ministry. Jesus' servant ministry is the model for all Christians. The words "ministry" and "service" are closely related. In its broadest sense, "ministry" denotes the service to which the whole people of God are called as individuals, as a local worshiping community of faith, or as the universal church. "Ministry" can also refer to the officially recognized forms this service can take within the church.

Your gifts as a baptized believer are vital to the church's mission, even though you may not be clear about what gifts you have received and how or where God is calling you to serve. The call to every Christian is the call to live out one's faith in service to the church and the world. All ministry in the church begins with the call to ministry in one's baptism.

God faithfully provides the persons needed and supplies the gifts required for the church to proclaim the powerful Easter message of Christ's resurrection. The church's ministry in the world is the ministry of that same risen Christ. The shape your particular ministry takes depends on the gifts and abilities given you by God as you live out your faith.

## THE MINISTRY OF THE BAPTIZED

*I believe that there is on earth a little holy flock or community of pure saints under one head, Christ. It is called together by the Holy Spirit in one faith, mind, and understanding. It possesses a variety of gifts, yet is united in*

> *love without sect or schism. Of this community I also am*
> *a part and member, a participant and co-partner in all*
> *the blessings it possesses.*[2]

Through the risen Christ, God calls all people into the "little holy flock" that proclaims the good news to a world in need of grace and new life. God first calls and empowers the church to extend the ministry of Jesus Christ in countless ways. *Vocation* is God's call at baptism to belong to God's family and to be a worker in the kingdom of God. The very word "vocation" is based on the word *vocatio*, which means "to be called." Individually, Christians are summoned to the Christian vocation as they live out their faith in the risen Christ in all dimensions of life—family, work, state, service to the neighbor, and care of creation. Martin Luther described the scope of vocation:

> *How is it possible that you are not called? You have*
> *always been in some state or station; you have always*
> *been a husband or wife, a boy or girl, or servant. . . . See,*
> *as no one is without some commission and calling, so no*
> *one is without some kind of work.*[3]

Occupations are only one avenue for Christian vocation. Discerning God's call involves clarity of one's abilities and gifts as well as attention to the needs of the world. Frederick Buechner describes this process of discernment:

> *By and large a good rule for finding out is this. The kind*
> *of work God usually calls you to is the kind of work (a)*
> *that you need most to do and (b) that the world most*
> *needs to have done. If you really get a kick out of your*
> *work, you've presumably met requirement (a), but if your*

*work is writing TV deodorant commercials, the chances
are you've missed requirement (b). On the other hand, if
your work is being a doctor in a leper colony, you have
probably met requirement (b), but if most of the time
you're bored and depressed by it, the chances are you have
not only bypassed (a) but probably aren't helping your
patients much either.*

*Neither the hair shirt nor the soft berth will do. The
place God calls you to is the place where your deep glad-
ness and the world's deep hunger meet.*[4]

## THE WHOLE PEOPLE OF GOD IN ACTION

Imagine the whole world as the arena in which Christians
use their various gifts in ministry. What would you see if
you watched them living out their vocation? You would
observe people of all nationalities, cultures, and abilities
gathered to hear the Word of God proclaimed, to share in
the Holy Communion, and to welcome the newly baptized
into Christ's church. Whether in a splendid edifice or a
makeshift store front, the baptized gather together in congregations to pray, sing, teach, learn, witness, and serve.
They are called by God and empowered by the Holy Spirit
to share in Christian worship and their life together.

You would also see the church scattered. God's people
care for the sick and the aged, advocate for justice and peace,
and stand with the poor and powerless of the world. Seven
days a week the church lives out its call with family, friends,
neighbors, strangers, and coworkers. Many use their
God-given gifts and abilities in the arenas of business, engineering, child care, science, farming, computers, education,
technology, social service, health care, and hundreds of
additional necessary occupations. There are students of all
ages, preparing for occupations or growing in continuing

education. There are many who have retired and who continue to be active members of their communities. Among
the baptized are also those who are called to serve in one of
the church's rostered ministries—as deaconesses, diaconal
ministers, associates in ministry, or pastors. In whatever
setting, all of the baptized are called to ministry in the
world for the sake of the gospel.

The varieties of settings for ministry challenge the baptized to live out their call faithfully. As you discern the
direction in which God may be calling you, we invite you to
consider how the Evangelical Lutheran Church in America
shapes its rostered ministries (ordained and lay) in order to
equip and support the ministry of the baptized in the world
and in this church.

## THE OFFICE OF MINISTRY: GOD'S GIFT TO THE CHURCH

How will the good news of the risen Christ be proclaimed?
How can the church care for and communicate this trea-
sure to all people at all times? The ministry of the gospel
has been entrusted to all believers. For the sake of that
gospel ministry, the Evangelical Lutheran Church in
America believes that God has instituted the office of ministry of Word and Sacrament. The faithful proclamation of
the gospel and the administration of the sacraments are
essential to the life of the church. Through this ministry,
the church proclaims God's promise that the risen Christ
alone justifies sinners by grace through faith apart from
works. The Augsburg Confession states the centrality of this
office:

> To obtain such faith God instituted the office of the min-
> istry, that is, provided the Gospel and the sacraments.
> Through these, as through means, he gives the Holy

> *Spirit, who works faith, when and where he pleases, in those who hear the Gospel.*[5]

·    The ministry of Jesus Christ is the foundation for all ministry. The baptized are called into ministry in the church and the world. Pastors, associates in ministry, deaconesses, and diaconal ministers serve to equip and support all the baptized.

> *". . . to equip the saints for the work of ministry, for building up the body of Christ, . . ."*
>
> Ephesians 4:12

## OFFICIALLY RECOGNIZED MINISTRIES OF THE EVANGELICAL LUTHERAN CHURCH IN AMERICA

To carry out Christ's ministry, the church calls from among the baptized those with leadership gifts to serve as ordained ministers (pastors and bishops) and as rostered laypersons (associates in ministry, deaconesses, and diaconal ministers). "Rostered" refers to the official list or roster that identifies people who meet certain standards set by this church for approval, accountability, and discipline. God calls these leaders through the church. They are not self-chosen or self-appointed.

The early Christians had no rosters, but leadership was urgently needed to proclaim the Word in both the present and the future. Throughout history God has called individuals to varied forms of ministry which came to be called "public ministry." Pastor-teachers, bishops, and deacons were called for the task of servant-leadership within the church to equip the baptized for their ministry in the world. Today the church continues to shape its ministries in order to bring the gospel to a changing world. In 1993, for example, the Evangelical Lutheran Church in America recognized diaconal ministry, which is linked to the biblical service of deacons, as a new form of rostered ministry.

*Called to serve.* The term "call" has many meanings. It refers to God's call in baptism to the whole church to extend the mission of Christ. "Call" is also the action of the church to set apart qualified persons for the ministry of Word and Sacrament, or for the ministries of associate in ministry, deaconess, or diaconal ministry. "Call" also refers to a decision by a congregation or other expression of this church to invite a qualified person to a specific rostered ministry. A "letter of call" then communicates the decision. Ordination, commissioning, and consecration are acts that are always dependent on such a call. People who meet requirements for preparation and are approved by a candidacy committee of this church are eligible to receive a letter of call to serve in one of the rostered ministries of the ELCA. Openness to call means willingness to serve wherever the church has need for a person's gifts.

The basic standards are the same for every person on this church's rosters:

- commitment to Christ;
- acceptance of and adherence to the Confession of Faith of this church;
- willingness and ability to serve in response to the needs of this church;
- academic and practical qualifications for ministry;
- life consistent with the Gospel and personal qualifications including leadership abilities and competence in interpersonal relationships;
- receipt and acceptance of a letter of call; and
- membership in a congregation of this church.

*Constitutions, Bylaws and Continuing Resolutions of the Evangelical Lutheran Church in America (7.31.11)*

God uses the rich varieties of gifts of our leaders in differing settings of ministry. Personalities of ordained ministers and rostered laypersons vary. Different settings and
forms of ministry call for different gifts and abilities for
ministry. Outgoing or reserved, energetic or reflective, tra-
ditional or creative—all may be found in leadership ministries. Intellectual or folksy, assertive or accommodating,
organized or spontaneous—each may have a place on the
official rosters if the gifts and the call are present.

## Ordained Ministers
## of Word and Sacrament: Pastors

*For, "Everyone who calls on the name of the Lord shall be
saved." But how are they to call on one in whom they
have not believed? And how are they to believe in one of
whom they have never heard? And how are they to hear
without someone to proclaim him?*

Romans 10:13-14

Pastors are baptized men and women whom the
Evangelical Lutheran Church in America calls and ordains
to the ministry of Word and Sacrament. On behalf of the
church, pastors give leadership and vision to Christian communities. A pastor is called to provide faithful preaching
and teaching of the Scriptures and the doctrinal tradition of
the Evangelical Lutheran Church in America. In preparation
for service, candidates for ordained ministry complete a
three-year master of divinity degree, normally from a seminary of the Evangelical Lutheran Church in America, and a
year of supervised internship. A candidate for ordained
ministry must be approved by a candidacy committee of
this church. The first call to ordained ministry in this
church is to be a pastor in a congregation. This church also
calls pastors to serve in other settings of ministry.

## PASTORS IN ACTION

The ministry of Word and Sacrament is at the heart of pastoral ministry. If you survey pastors at work, you will observe a variety of activities with many styles and within different cultures, yet all are anchored in the ministry of Word and Sacrament. Most pastors in this church serve in small congregations in rural, suburban, or urban contexts, but the message to communities of every size is the same: "Christ has died. Christ is risen! Christ will come again!" These pastors preach the Christian message every week in fresh ways, stirring up faith in the community. They preside at the celebration of Holy Communion, saying, "The body of Christ, given for you. The blood of Christ, shed for you." Pastors pour the waters of baptism on new brothers and sisters, then walk with them through the years as they discern the meaning of this baptismal call. They stand at the graveside to declare Jesus' words: "I am the resurrection and the life. . . . Whoever lives and believes in me shall never die."

Pastors pray, study, and teach. Sitting on the floor with children or perched behind a lectern in an inquirer's class, pastors teach the Word of God and its implications for every stage of life. They may be instruments of God's reconciling grace to a broken family or catalysts to inspire the people of their congregation to reach out to the homeless. They lead the congregation in stewardship of resources, both human and material, and in evangelism. They enable congregations to speak faithfully and firmly in matters of conflict and controversy. They work in partnership with other rostered ministers called to serve in the ministries of this church and with lay leaders in congregations and synods.

Pastoral ministry is filled with paradox and opportunity. One afternoon a pastor may pray with a person suffering in the last stage of cancer in a hospital, and a few hours later celebrate a wedding with a man and a woman and their families. Pastors in this church are called to speak publicly on behalf of the church to the world in solidarity with the poor and oppressed, calling for justice and proclaiming God's love for the world. As they speak, the church moves into the world in the name of the risen Christ to bring about justice and peace.

The church calls pastors to particular settings in which they are evangelists in door-to-door mission development. Pastors serve in areas where a Lutheran witness is needed, as well as in small congregations that are discouraged by declining membership. They lead congregations in isolated locations inside and far beyond the cities, as well as in dynamic congregations in suburban, small-town, and rural settings.

The Evangelical Lutheran Church in America has called one in five of its active ordained pastors to serve the needs of the church in the care of the gospel in settings outside the congregation. Supported by and accountable to this church, these pastors extend the ministry of Word and Sacrament into specialized settings in health care and social service agencies; in colleges and seminaries; in camps and missionary fields; and in synodical, regional, and church-wide offices.

## Bishops

One ordained minister is called to serve as presiding bishop of the Evangelical Lutheran Church in America. This bishop's primary responsibility is to be a teacher of the faith and to provide leadership for the life and witness of this church. Each synod also calls a bishop to lead the life and mission of the synod and oversee its work. You will find these bishops preaching, teaching, and administering the sacraments throughout congregations and at assemblies. As pastors provide pastoral leadership for congregations, bishops offer the same for their synod. Bishops play a distinctive role as ecumenical officers who are called to serve the unity of the church with other denominations.

## ROSTERED LAY MINISTERS

*For as in one body we have many members, and not all the members have the same function, so we, who are many, are one body in Christ, and individually we are members one of another. We have gifts that differ according to the grace given to us.*

Romans 12:4-5

Laypersons also play a vital role in the leadership ministry of the Evangelical Lutheran Church in America. The church calls theologically educated and professionally qualified laypersons to employ their differing gifts as leaders to support and extend the ministry of Word and Sacrament among all the people of God. Settings and activities of rostered laypersons may resemble those of some ordained ministers. A congregation or other calling entity determines which form of rostered ministry is most appropriate for a given setting of ministry. The primary focus of each form is distinct yet complementary with the ordained, other lay rosters, and the ministry of the whole church. Because the forms of lay ministry are flexible, qualified persons are able to respond creatively to challenges the church identifies.

Leadership for witness and service as an extension of the ministry of Word and Sacrament is at the heart of rostered lay ministry. Diaconal ministers, deaconesses, and associates in ministry are the three forms of lay ministries officially recognized on rosters of this church. While tasks in the three categories may overlap, each form has a unique history, different preparation, and a distinct focus. All enhance the mission of the church in significant ways. A few examples follow to suggest the scope of lay ministries in the Evangelical Lutheran Church in America.

## ROSTERED LAYPERSONS IN ACTION

You will find rostered laypersons working in partnership with pastors and bishops to equip the baptized for ministry in the church and in the world. Most frequently they are part of the staff in congregations where they provide leadership as well as support for the programmatic ministries of the church. Musicians enhance the church's liturgy and worship so that the church can sing the gospel's "new song." Christian educators develop and implement the teaching ministry of the church to communicate the gospel to every age level. Christian day school teachers carry out the critical ministry of education to the young, as well as participate in the church's outreach to the community.

Others respond to God's call by using their administrative gifts to care for the church's resources and to involve members in stewardship of life. Those who specialize in family, youth, and children's ministries design opportunities to bring the good news into daily life. Rostered laypersons extend the church's ministry as parish nurses, program coordinators, and outreach directors. Some serve as catechists and evangelists, advocates of justice, editors, and communicators. Others will be found teaching at all levels, counseling; providing health care; and administering in camps, agencies, and institutions. Some assist bishops in synodical and churchwide work.

## DIACONAL MINISTERS

Diaconal minister is a form of ministry officially established by the Evangelical Lutheran Church in America in 1993. It is a ministry that shares with deaconesses a common heritage. The roots of diaconal ministry go back to the early church. The term "diaconal" comes from the Greek word *diakonia* which means "service" or "ministry." In the early church, members of the diaconate (who were usually called deacons) read the Gospels, assisted with the eucharistic meal, and led the congregation in prayer and in service to the poor. The Evangelical Lutheran Church in America calls diaconal ministers to positions that exemplify the servant life and that seek to equip and motivate others to live it. In a great variety of ways, they empower, equip, and support all the baptized people of God in the ministry of Jesus Christ and the mission of God in the world. While the pulpit, font, and chalice are symbols of pastoral ministry, the basin and towel are at the heart of diaconal ministry (John 13:1-20).

Word, service, and witness are central to diaconal ministry. Diaconal service reflects the historic call of deacons to serve those most in need at personal and societal levels on behalf of the church, crossing the boundaries between the church and the world. Diaconal ministers are called to exemplify Christ-like service wherever human need and the gospel message intersect.

Diaconal ministers are people professionally trained in an area of expertise to insure competence in their field, such as social work, counseling, teaching, law, or medicine. All diaconal ministers complete a first professional degree from a seminary, such as master of arts, master of theological studies, or master of arts in religion. In addition, a candidate must complete supervised field work and a program in Lutheran diaconal formation, and participate in the ELCA candidacy process.

With such preparation, diaconal ministers speak for the needs of God's world to the church and carry God's saving gospel to the needs of the world. Diaconal ministers may work as evangelists among groups usually untouched by the gospel. They speak on behalf of the church as advocates for justice, as social workers, or as counselors, for example. Diaconal ministers do not carry out this ministry alone, but are called to lead and equip others for "diakonia" (witness and service) in the world.

When diaconal ministers work in congregations, they seek ways to extend the witness of the church into the wider community. They work with the baptized in discerning gifts and equip them for service within and beyond the congregation. Their calls may be to serve in the ministry of education, mission and evangelism, care, administration, or music and the arts.

Diaconal ministry is grounded in a community of support and shared vision. The diaconal community, developed and nurtured through formation, serves as an anchor and as a reminder to build community wherever one is called, in congregations and other settings.

## The Deaconess Community of the Evangelical Lutheran Church in America

For more than one hundred years, deaconesses serving in North America have complemented the ministry of Word and Sacrament and the ministry of the whole people of God. Deaconesses are a vital part of the diaconate, which through the centuries in the church catholic has extended the ministry of Jesus in areas of service. This rich heritage is carried on by the Deaconess Community of the Evangelical Lutheran Church in America and by members in the Evangelical Lutheran Church in America who belong to the Lutheran Deaconess Association. The Deaconess

Community of the ELCA is a specific roster in this church. Members of the Lutheran Deaconess Association, an independent deaconess organization, who are members of and serve within the ELCA, are rostered either as associates in ministry or diaconal ministers. Historically, deaconesses have initiated ministries in social service and health care along with missionary work, education, and congregational service. These roots prepare them for expanded service in innovative ways to address needs the church may recognize. The Deaconess Community of the Evangelical Lutheran Church in America, while similar in vision and mission to diaconal ministers, is distinguished by the specific commitment to serve as an intentional community of women. Each deaconess candidate spends a period of time participating in the life of the community and pursuing diaconal and theological studies.

Deaconess candidates are expected to have a degree in their field of expertise, then to complete a course of theological studies at an Evangelical Lutheran Church in America seminary, usually a master of arts in religion or the equivalent. Candidates become "sisters" and may be consecrated to the office of deaconess after being approved by a candidacy committee and accepting an appropriate call.

Skilled and committed women, who may be married, act in community to complement the ministry of Word and Sacrament and all God's people. In recent years, members of the community have served in a wide range of calls, often related to serving women and their children. They have extended the good news in the health care field as a midwife in Appalachia, research nurse for a pediatric AIDS clinic, nurse to children of drug-addicted mothers, and professional foster parent for medically needy infants. Others have served as a church publications editor, assistant to the bishop, director of a children's performing arts company, and parish deaconess. Deaconesses often live in the community with the people they serve as a living presence of the message of the gospel.

Deaconesses experience a unique relationship with other members of the Deaconess Community. The community supports its members through preparation for service and through spiritual, personal, and professional growth. It assists deaconesses when they are seeking calls, supports them throughout their ministry, and serves them in retirement. The Deaconess Community of this church is related to the worldwide diaconate.

## ASSOCIATES IN MINISTRY

The term "associate in ministry" helps define the character of this officially recognized lay ministry. An associate is a partner, an ally who equips others to carry out a goal, sometimes taking the lead and on other occasions working in a support role. For decades the churches that joined together to form the Evangelical Lutheran Church in America had developed a wide variety of recognized lay ministries with diverse background and training. "Associate in ministry" was designated as the official name for all the inherited rosters at the beginning of the Evangelical Lutheran Church in America and continues as a category of ministry in the life of this church today. Those who now serve under this broad category represent a thriving tradition of rostered lay ministries.

Associates in ministry provide leadership to this church through programmatic ministries in congregations as well as in agencies and institutions of the church. Associates in ministry may be found bringing leadership and expertise in a variety of settings throughout the ELCA.

To be approved for commissioning by a candidacy committee, candidates must complete a minimum of a bachelor's degree and demonstrate competency in one of four designated fields: education, music and the arts, administration, or service and general ministries. They complete supervised field experience and twenty semester hours in theological education in approved courses at a college, seminary, or by extension. Associate in ministry candidates who are approved by a candidacy committee may be commissioned to use their gifts in service after receiving a letter of call from a congregation or a church-related agency or institution.

Currently, associates in ministry may be found in differing settings. Educators include those who serve as directors of Christian education, Lutheran school and college teachers and administrators, seminary professors, and youth ministry directors. The ministry of music and the arts is extended by directors of church music, teachers of music, liturgical artists, and cantors. Associates in ministry carry out the ministry of administration as business administrators in congregations, in synods as assistants to bishops, and in churchwide institutions and agencies. Service and general ministries are open-ended to encourage leadership ministry in areas both in and beyond the congregation. Parish nurse, social worker, church-related career counselor, outdoor or campus minister, and drug and alcohol counselor are but a few calls of those who serve as associates in ministry.

## FOR REFLECTION

- Pray for the presence and guidance of the Holy Spirit.
- Think about experiences you have had in congregations and in church-related activities. What images come to mind? What moments stand out? What people touched or influenced you? What gifts for ministry were needed and present?
- In what ways do you perceive God present in these occasions?
- As you read the brief descriptions of varieties of ministries, which activities energized you most—those of the ministry of the baptized, of ordained ministry, or of rostered laypersons?
- As you read the descriptions of varieties of ministries in the ELCA, what questions do you have? Do you need more information?

*Blessed are you,*
*O Lord our God, maker of all things. Through your good-*
*ness you have blessed us with these gifts. With them we*
*offer ourselves to your service and dedicate our lives to the*
*care and redemption of all that you have made, for the*
*sake of him who gave himself for us, Jesus Christ our*
*Lord. Amen.*

*Lutheran Book of Worship*, Holy Communion

"Follow me, and I will make you fish for people." Immediately they left their nets and followed him. (Jesus to Simon and Andrew.)
Matthew 4:19,20

For as in one body we have many members, and not all the members have the same function, so we, who are many, are one body in Christ, and individually we are members one of another. We have gifts that differ according to the grace given to us.
Romans 12:4–6

# CHAPTER 3

# *Discerning God's Call and God's Gifts*

*"F*ollow me" is an invitation to travel with Jesus into the world. Just how to follow Jesus through life's journey is critical. Some have followed into ministries within the context of daily life, such as educators, engineers, or salespersons. Others have followed into ministries within the context of the institutional church, such as ordained pastors or rostered lay ministers. In each case, following Jesus promises a lifetime of opportunities for joy in witness and love through obedience.

Jesus gives the gift of ministry to the whole church and calls each baptized sister and brother to swim in the marvelous gift of grace. For, "each of us was given grace according to the measure of Christ's gift" (Ephesians 4:7). The question is not, "Do you have gifts for ministry?" The question is, "What gifts do you have for which ministry?" To which ministry is the Holy Spirit calling you? What gifts has the triune God created into your very being for you to use as you follow Jesus? Your answers are deeply personal, and at the same time, rooted in the Christian community.

We have spoken of "calls" and "calling." But just what is a "call," and what does "being called" mean? Is this just religious jargon for career decisions, job placements, changes of employment? We want to think of the word "call" in connection with the word "discernment." In this chapter we will begin by distinguishing "discernment" from "career decisions" as a way to begin understanding the meaning of "call." Then we will identify our basic call as God's call that is extended to all Christians through baptism. Finally, we will consider "call" in terms of ordained and rostered lay ministries in the church.

## DISCERNMENT AND GIFTS

Discernment is the dynamic process of discovering God's call in every dimension of life. The process incorporates the whole person—head and heart, passion and logic, faith and doubt, challenge and mystery. More specifically, discernment invites you to explore whether you are being called by the triune God for ordained or rostered ministries in the church or whether God needs you to invest your talents to serve in other arenas of life.

Discernment is grounded in Jesus' farewell discourse to the disciples:

> *You did not choose me but I chose you. And I appointed you to go and bear fruit, fruit that will last, so that the Father will give you whatever you ask him in my name. I am giving you these commands so that you may love one another.*
>
> John 15:16-17

To discern God's call means to discover what God has already decided for the church in the world: namely, that every Christian, chosen at baptism, "may proclaim the praise of God and bear his creative and redeeming Word to all the world" (*Lutheran Book of Worship*, Holy Baptism, p. 124). God does the choosing, not the individual. The story of Jesus' mission as written in the four Gospels of the New Testament describes those who faithfully seek to live out their calling, their vocation.

Discernment takes as many shapes as there are seekers. Some perceive God's call in dramatic, even mystical experiences, while others detect God's voice in the ordinariness of life. While some interpret God's call and analyze their gifts quite rationally, others may anguish or be ecstatic about their spiritual journey. Two characteristics remain constant: discerning the call and discerning gifts are bonded together in the individual and in the church.

Discerning God's call and discerning God's gifts are two separate but interrelated dimensions. Major clues to the direction God is calling you may be discovered in particular abilities and qualities that may be transformed into gifts in ministry. The call to share in Jesus' vision for mission is fundamental, but it is incomplete without honest insights into abilities and qualities that may be needed. At the same time, a person may possess remarkable abilities but may not grasp the radical vision of the church. God's call and gifts play off each other in creative tension through discernment.

## DISCERNMENT AND DECISION MAKING

Discernment and decision making are distinctly different yet related approaches to responding to God's call. Decision makers define the problem, gather data, analyze options, weigh pros and cons, then cut away all choices but one. While other people may be consulted, the power of choice lies basically in the hands of the decision maker. This is appropriate for many kinds of decisions, such a making a major purchase or deciding which college to attend.

It might seem as if this is also appropriate for making a decision about ordained or rostered lay ministry. Someone who is considering rostered ministry might analyze personal strengths and weaknesses, evaluate the fit with various job descriptions in the church, then decide to become a pastor or a diaconal minister, for example.

In the United States we can see this in the way that talented individuals have established their own "ministries," often using their own names to identify their ministries, and almost always establishing their ministries apart from the churches or traditions with which they might, in some loose way, be identified. Their powerful personal sense of call seems to have little to do with the church.

Such an approach can be dangerous for the people who respond to such ministries as well as for the individuals who engage in them. Well-meaning people have been manipulated, exploited, deceived, cheated, and, in some instances, led to despair and death by charismatic individuals, religious charlatans, and self-willed individuals who have been grasped and driven by something quite other than the gospel.

Yet, in the Lutheran tradition an individual's discernment is only a part of the process. An authentic call to ordained or rostered lay ministry involves the church as well as the individual. Hence the church initiates the call, and tests the sense of call and the needed gifts for its ordained and rostered lay ministries. It has both the right and the responsibility to do so. The very notion of self-appointed and self-proclaimed leaders contradicts what it means to be a leader in the church. It is also precisely what "heresy" means: going your own way, on your own terms, with yourself as your own authority. "Orthodoxy" means rightly, authentically, praising God and rightly, authentically, teaching the gospel. Right teaching of the gospel takes place when the church teaches the gospel in accordance with Holy Scripture and the classic creeds and confessions. It is not one person's homemade version of God's truth.

## God's Call through Baptism

Baptism is the basic call to the church and to all of its individual members. In baptism we are grasped and enfolded by the great saving event of Jesus' cross and resurrection.

That is the meaning of the washing with water "in the name of the Father, and the Son, and the Holy Spirit."

A "name" identifies the particular history of a person. "Harriet Tubman" means nothing until you learn that she was an escaped slave who led many slaves to freedom on the Underground Railroad prior to the freeing of all slaves at the end of the American Civil War. "Father, Son, and Holy Spirit" identifies the history of God, which has the resurrection of Jesus as its starting point and the cross of Jesus as its focus.

In the cross Jesus suffered our death at the hands of sinners like us. Humans crucified Jesus because, under the power of death and sin, we reject God's audacious insistence on *unconditional* mercy and love. It is too radical for those of us who insist on justifying our own existence on our terms, too sweeping for those of us who despair of any justification for our existence.

In the cross, the one Jesus called "Father" suffers by handing over to death the Son who is utterly and eternally loved by and united with his Father. In the cross the Holy Spirit of life and hope *endures* the cost of overcoming death and despair so that nothing can now defeat the Creator Spirit's life and hope.

Thus, to be baptized into the "name of the Father, Son, and Holy Spirit" is to be baptized into the one event in all of history that offers and guarantees salvation and hope. All of us who have been baptized into Christ have put on Christlike clothing (Galatians 3:27 and Colossians 3:10), and through him we "have access in one Spirit to the Father" (Ephesians 2:18). We are therefore free to acknowledge our calling to be one new humanity (Galatians 3:28; Ephesians 4:1-6; Colossians 3:11), to deal with each other honestly and truthfully (Colossians 3:9), to live by faith and not by sight (2 Corinthians 4:16-18). In all of this we are given both the freedom and the call to live in terms of Jesus' way of being in the world.

This act of the baptizing God takes place through the church. In baptism the church baptizes us into the name and faith of the triune God. In baptism the church, through sponsors, promises to care for and help *in every way* those whom it baptizes (*Lutheran Book of Worship*, Holy Baptism, p. 122). This is an act of grace and promise that makes the church different from every other human community. The church's commitment is unconditional and forever because God's commitment is unconditional and forever!

Thus, the whole church is called through baptism to represent and embody God's unconditional commitment to the world. When the church celebrates the Holy Communion, it is celebrating the eternal banquet of the Messiah (Matthew 8:11), a "foretaste of the feast to come" (*Lutheran Book of Worship*, Holy Communion, p. 66). We share in the body that Christ offered for the world so that we become the body of Christ for the world (1 Corinthians 11:17-34). We want "to receive him always with thanksgiving, and to conform our lives to his" (*Lutheran Book of Worship*, Holy Communion, p. 74).

That is what gives expression and shape to the church's witness, its witness to the resurrection of Jesus, its witness that life and not death will have the last word. The love of God in Christ Jesus calls the church; and this call is to every member of the church. This unconditional love is the basis for our callings in the world. Every Christian is called and challenged, empowered and obligated to struggle with the meaning of unconditional love in the marketplace and street, in the world of conflicting interests and brute power. Christians are called to represent the reign of God in a world where death and sin are still powerfully operative.

## THE CALL TO MINISTRIES IN THE CHURCH

Upholding the calls of the baptized in a time and place
where the reign of death and sin continues to challenge is
the calling of ordained and rostered lay ministries in the
Evangelical Lutheran Church in America. What does such a
calling in the church mean? We look to Holy Scripture and
to the experiences of a few individuals in the church's
history for examples and insight.

Scripture overflows with stories of God seeking out and
working through young people like Miriam and Jeremiah,
as well as turning around lives in midstream, as with Peter
and Mary Magdalene. Moses, Samuel, David, Deborah,
Naomi and Ruth, Isaiah, Jeremiah, Mary, the twelve disciples, Mary of Bethany, Paul, Lydia, and Priscilla demonstrate the various ways some servants have used their gifts
to follow God's call. The gifts God showered on these leaders fit their ages, context, and the urgent needs of God's
people.

One characteristic of many call stories is *resistance* to
the call. Jeremiah responds to his call with the objection
that he is too young (Jeremiah 1:6); Isaiah objects that he is
"a man of unclean lips" (Isaiah 6:5). One of the most celebrated examples of resistance, of course, is described in the
story of Jonah. It is the story of a runaway who sets out in
the direction opposite to God's call. Even when he eventually arrives at the destination to which God called him, he
must learn that God's purpose is mercy, not punishment.

Some calls have been dramatic and sudden, involving a
radical change in life. St. Paul was on his way to Damascus
to continue his persecution of disciples of Jesus when he
was struck down by blinding light and the voice of the
Lord. He continued his journey to Damascus, but there he
was baptized and became the great missionary apostle
(Acts 9:1-31). Martin Luther was studying to become a

lawyer when a thunderstorm overtook him at Stotternheim
as he was walking back to the university at Erfurt. In a
moment of physical and spiritual terror he vowed to
become a monk. John Newton (1725-1807), author of the
hymn "Amazing Grace," was a slave trader until 1755. His
wife, Mary, had given him a copy of the book *The Imitation
of Christ*, and he was reading it when a storm nearly sank
his ship. Within a few years he was an ordained priest who
wrote this inscription about himself at his second parish
church, St. Mary Woolnoth, in London:

> *John Newton, Clerk,*
> *Once an infidel and libertine,*
> *A servant of slaves in Africa,*
> *Was, by the rich mercy of our Lord*
> *And Savior Jesus Christ,*
> *Preserved, restored, pardoned,*
> *And appointed to preach the Faith*
> *He had long labored to destroy,*
> *Near sixteen years at Olney in Bucks,*
> *And twenty-eight years in this church.*[6]

One of the features of many calls is that persons seem to
hear the very voice of God. Samuel hears an unwelcome
word of God in the middle of the night. (1 Samuel 3:10-14)
The description of Mary's call to be the mother of Jesus
(Luke 1:26-39) was both mystical and terrifying for the
young girl. The messenger tells her not to be afraid,
patiently answers her perplexity and her questions. Finally,
with great courage, Mary replies, "Here am I, the servant of
the Lord; let it be with me according to your word."
     St. Augustine (A.D. 354–430), one of the great theolo-
gians of the Western church, heard a voice in a garden in
Milan telling him to "take up and read." His reading of

Romans 13:12-14 led to his baptism and his return to Africa. There he struggled against the very idea of ordained ministry by avoiding cities where there was no bishop. Attending a liturgy in Hippo-Regius one Sunday, he was physically brought forward and ordained by Bishop Valerius, who had announced in his sermon that he needed an assistant!

Most persons, however, experience a call to ministry in less dramatic or mystical ways. St. Timothy, to whom two letters of the New Testament are addressed, was brought up by a pious mother, Eunice, and a pious grandmother, Lois (2 Timothy 1:5). St. Paul met him in Lystra (Acts 16:1) and called Timothy by inviting him to become his companion in St. Paul's own mission journeys. If there was any drama involved, we aren't told. We do not know how Junia became an apostle (Romans 16:7), or how Phoebe became a deacon (Romans 16:1). We know only that Junia and her colleague Andronicus were "prominent among the apostles" at Rome. We know only that Phoebe had been "a benefactor of many" and of St. Paul himself. The Greek word that is translated "benefactor" does not mean that Phoebe was an "aide" to the great apostle, but that she was a *patron*, a *protector*!

The very ordinary ways in which the call comes to you might be the persistent encouragement of some member of your family, or the suggestion of your parish pastor or your campus minister that you consider visiting a seminary. You may have met a student in your college who comes from another continent and who fills you with excitement about the global character of the church. You may have learned about some courageous Christian like Dietrich Bonhoeffer (1905–1945), Martin Luther King Jr. (1929–1968), or Mother Teresa (1910–1997), whose example inspires you.

Perhaps you have come to enjoy reading and studying theology in college classes. You may have been influenced by the example of a pastor, youth worker, your mother or your father, an aunt or an uncle. Or you may have always "known" that you wanted to be a pastor, deaconess, associate in ministry, or diaconal minister. Perhaps you have simply experienced a sense of fulfillment in teaching a church school class or serving a term on the church council. Or you may have enjoyed speaking with the person who represented a seminary at a churchwide youth gathering.

Nothing dramatic. Nothing mystical. Just the steady perception or the growing recognition that this is a future that you must explore and investigate.

### SHARING THE VISION OF JESUS

The important factor in a call is not the circumstance through which one experiences a call, but how one understands the *content* and *character* of the ministry to which one is called. Ordained and rostered lay ministers in the church have an authentic call when they trust and use the gifts given to them when they were baptized. They discover that they are compelled to share the vision that Jesus' way of being in and for the world is the way the church is called to be in and for the world.

Those who are called and authorized to speak and act for God in the world share in Jesus' "cup" and Jesus' "baptism."

> *The cup that I drink you will drink; and with the baptism with which I am baptized, you will be baptized; but to sit at my right hand or at my left is not mine to grant. . . . You know that those who are supposed to rule over the Gentiles lord it over them, and their great men exercise authority over them. But it shall not be so among you; but whoever would be great among you must be your servant, and*

*whoever would be first among you must be slave of all. For
the Son of man also came not to be served but to serve,
and to give his life as ransom for many.*

Mark 10:39-45

The authentic call that authorizes public ministry occurs
only where there is freedom conferred by Jesus' resurrection to share in the baptismal mission of Christ. People
have an authentic call to ordained and rostered lay ministry
in the church when they have been grasped by that vision.
Others, grasped by the same vision, will understand that
their call is to ministry in daily life.

The blessing of God is that you are not left to draw
your own conclusions about the authenticity of your call.
You do not have to spend time worrying about whether
your call is authentic. Your call will be tested again and
again by the church.

The call by God to rostered ministry comes from a
community of Christians who want you to exercise the gift
of ministry in its midst and on its behalf. If so you will be
ordained, consecrated, or commissioned, with prayer for
the Holy Spirit and with the hands of your predecessors
laid on your head, just as Paul and Barnabas were called
and sent by the church in Syrian Antioch so long ago
(Acts 13:1-3).

If the time finally comes that the church sets you apart
for ordained or rostered lay ministry, you will not be asked
about the strength of your own sense of call. You will be
asked whether you believe that the church's call is God's
call!

### FOR REFLECTION:

- Begin to consider and name "what gifts the triune God created into your very being."

- Reflect on moments you have heard or sensed God's call. When are you most receptive to listening to God? In quiet meditation? In conversation with others? During worship?

- Reflect on important decisions you have made. How do you normally approach decision making? How can you enter into "discernment"? Who or what do you need to assist you in this process?

- Reflect on your baptism. Read through the service of Holy Baptism on page 121 of *Lutheran Book of Worship*. How does the power of baptism affect your everyday life?

*Send now, we pray, your Holy Spirit,*
*the spirit of our Lord and of his resurrection,*
*that we who receive the Lord's body and blood*
*may live to the praise of your glory*
*and receive our inheritance*
*with all your saints in light.*

*Amen. Come, Holy Spirit.*

*Lutheran Book of Worship*, Holy Communion

"Do not let your hearts be troubled. Believe in God, believe also in me." . . . Thomas said to [Jesus], "Lord, we do not know where you are going. How can we know the way?" Jesus said to him, "I am the way, and the truth, and the life."

John 14:1, 5–6

# CHAPTER 4    *Paths to Discernment*

The church is on the move, eager to extend the message of the risen Christ to a broken world. Early Christians were identified as "those who belong to the Way," as those who followed Jesus' way of being in the world (Acts 9:2). As a follower of Christ today, you are called to discover the way and the will of God for your life. Even though you may be uncertain about the specific character of God's will for you, you are not alone in your search. For centuries, pilgrims before you have wrestled to be obedient to God's call. Based on their experiences, several paths for discernment offer general guidance for you to adapt to your particular journey.

Discernment is the process of perceiving what already exists in the will of God for the church and for the people. God does the choosing and the calling, and Christians respond. The six paths or approaches that follow may help you as you discover the full meaning of being called as a child of God.

- Worship, study, and pray with the church.
- Talk with people who know you.
- Seek pastoral and spiritual guidance.
- Explore work in the church and in other occupations.
- Discern gifts for ministry.
- Respond to God's call in faith and obedience.

These interdependent and overlapping dimensions of discernment are not to be taken in sequence like steps to be completed; rather, they are facets of a lifelong course that you and the church take together. They are interwoven like a tapestry, reflecting the responsibility that you and the church carry in discerning whether you do indeed have a call to rostered ministry in the church or to another arena. An excerpt from *Vision and Expectations,* a document that describes this church's expectations of those who serve in rostered ministry, highlights issues that are valid for every Christian:

> *It is the awareness of the Gospel in one's life, and the response to that Gospel, that lead some to seek to serve in the public ministry of the church. This call may include the example and encouragement of others, the personal assessment of an individual's own interests and abilities, and response to the needs of the world. Whatever way the call . . . may come to an individual, the Evangelical Lutheran Church in America believes that such a sense of call must be tested over a period of time, shaped by theological study, and finally confirmed in the church's call.*
>
> Vision and Expectations, p. 5

## WORSHIP, STUDY, AND PRAY WITH THE CHURCH

Discernment begins and ends on one's knees, where God's calling voice may be heard and tested. Here the struggle to obey is engaged. The gift of faith that seeks understanding is nurtured and stimulated through worship, Bible study, and prayer in God's family as well as individual prayer. Frequent attention to the Word proclaimed and participation in Holy Communion, along with the prayers of the people, are critical in discernment. Each time the community gathers to celebrate Holy Communion, be aware of the meaning of the offertory prayer:

> *Merciful Father, we offer with joy and thanksgiving what you have first given us—our selves, our time, and our possessions, signs of your gracious love. Receive them for*

*the sake of him who offered himself for us, Jesus Christ
our Lord. Amen.*

*Lutheran Book of Worship*, Holy Communion

Pray not only for guidance and direction in God's will, but
also pray for the whole church, the nations, those in need,
the congregation, and special concerns. Pray for openness
to perceive what God is doing in the world, in the church,
and in your own life. Seek clarity in the paradoxes of life
lived in the shadow of the cross and in the certain hope of
the resurrection. Above all, remember God's promises,
Martin Luther's favorite word for the gospel. Ask what is
God's future, what is God's hope for the world, and how
you can extend the gifts of God in service to that future.

Prayer in the name of Jesus means the struggle to discern God's will for the church and for your place in the
church. If your prayer attempts to manipulate God to get
what you wanted in the first place, you may reach out to
others to help you pray more as Jesus prayed. His prayer in
Gethsemane is a model for discerning God's will: "yet, not
what I want, but what you want" (Mark 14:36).

## TALK WITH PEOPLE WHO KNOW YOU

Discernment is a communal process. St. Paul explains that
we are one body in Christ, and individually we are members one of another (Romans 12:3-8). God is incarnational,
often sounding remarkably like the voice of a parent, pastor, director of Christian education, teacher, or professor.
Because self-deception is a risk while pursuing self-insight,
other people may assist you in distinguishing God's call
from your own wishes and from the voices around you.

*Talk with people with different perspectives.* Talk not only to
those who already share your self-perceptions, but also to

people who will surprise you, who will challenge you, who love you enough to help you see yourself more truly than you are able to see yourself on your own. Invite them to mirror with care and honesty what gifts they perceive in you and what arenas they imagine you might serve for Christ's sake in the church and in the world. Encourage them to help you recognize your weaknesses and growing edges.

*Talk with your family.* Talk honestly and openly with your family at every point in your discernment process. The more directly your decisions affect them, the more critical it is that they be involved in future planning. You may invite your pastor or some other leader to meet with you and your family so that your growing perception of God's will for the church and for yourself also includes them.

## SEEK PASTORAL AND SPIRITUAL GUIDANCE

Speak with leaders in the church for prayerful guidance. Include your pastor or college chaplain, as well as others whose faith and wisdom inspire you—diaconal ministers, deaconesses, associates in ministry, teachers, lay leaders. Share with your pastor and others the nudges you may be receiving; the questions you bring; and the hopes you have for life, the church, and the world. These leaders will be able to listen, to accept you, to affirm you in the midst of faith and doubt, and to pray with you for discernment of and obedience to God's will. Hear them talk about the joys and trials of their journeys. Learn how they prepared for leadership in the church and ask what steps are needed if you become a candidate for ordained or rostered lay ministry.

Discerning God's call is not a one-time event. Choices are revisited at crossroads throughout life, both by individuals and by the church. As on any path, you walk toward discernment only one step at a time. For example, just because you decide to attend one year of seminary does not automatically mean that you or the church will want you to continue in preparation for rostered ministry. Nor does a choice to enter a different occupation prevent you from preparing for rostered ministry later in your life. It is important to remember that by opening up the possibility of call you may discover that God is calling you to some challenge quite different from the one you expect. Your pastor in particular will help you remember your baptism, walk with you no matter what the outcome, and uphold you with Word and Sacrament.

Another resource person for discernment may be a spiritual director. The term refers to people with specific training in guiding a person in nurturing their relationship with God in all aspects of life through prayer. Spiritual direction has roots in the tradition of the church catholic. Pastors, rostered laypersons, and other church leaders may also be trained in this discipline. Spiritual directors guide you to find yourself in the heart of God, and then to discover what is in God's heart for you and others. They will help you listen to and understand your inner self so that you can distinguish between God's voice and the other voices within you. Spiritual directors help you find courage to face the gifts and graces received as well as the blind spots that block abundant living. Furthermore, spiritual direction points toward the future and encompasses the whole of life across the life span rather than focusing on a one-time decision.

Seek the guidance of your synod bishop or a member of the bishop's staff. It is a responsibility of the bishop to have a concern for the next generation of leaders in the church, both those on official rosters and others. The bishop or bishop's staff will be able to tell you about the mission needs of congregations, agencies, institutions, and mission fields. Without knowing your particular gifts, the bishop can describe qualities the church needs for leadership ministries. Ask about the availability of discernment retreats or "Invitation to Service" gatherings. Keep in touch with the bishop as your journey progresses.

The leaders named above can help you determine when and how to begin the candidacy process for rostered ministry in the Evangelical Lutheran Church in America. The entrance phase, which begins in the congregation, is designed both for people who are very tentative about their call (the "seeker") and for those who have discerned a call to ordained or rostered lay ministry. Interviews and career counseling will further assist you in the discernment process that you and the church both share. Additional information about candidacy in the Evangelical Lutheran Church in America is covered in Chapter 5.

## EXPLORE WORK IN THE CHURCH AND IN OTHER OCCUPATIONS

*Survey varieties of ministry.* Broaden your vision of Christ's church beyond that of your own experience. Visit large and small, rural and urban, mission and long-established congregations in the full range of ethnic and cultural diversity that comprises the Evangelical Lutheran Church in America. Learn more about ministries in the church's agencies and institutions. Discover the significant relationships among churches worldwide. The church's ministry may be far broader and the varieties of service far greater than you now realize.

*Test possibilities in leadership ministries.* Test the potential call to rostered ministry and to other realms by seeking supervised experiences. There is no substitute for trying to understand and to experience what leadership ministry is like from the inside. The process will help you determine whether you may have gifts of leadership, which are not the same as the ability to help people or to do public speaking well. Walking through the actual tasks with someone who is already doing them can help you recognize if you have the ability to give vision to a community and to lead a community to carry out Christ's vision. Ask to be trained to assist in your congregation or a church-related agency or institution. You might provide leadership in worship, teach, write, visit, and use specialized gifts you may have. Find mentors who work in areas that intrigue you, such as a pastor, campus minister, or church musician, to name a few.

*Investigate other settings for Christian service.* The period of exploration is an ideal time to examine the many activities to which God calls people. With your pastor or others, identify Christians who use their gifts in service in areas of additional interest to you, such as education, health care, law, science, technology, or business. Ask permission to be with them for a day to experience the abilities their work demands and to appreciate the contributions they make. Listen to them tell how they live out their vocation in daily life. Explore how well your gifts and potential seem to meet their job descriptions. For more intensive experience, seek part-time service or an internship in a ministry setting.

## DISCERN GIFTS FOR MINISTRY

Prayer and worship, conversations, pastoral and spiritual guidance, and experience in various settings all lead to the central question, "What gifts do I have for which ministry?"

Paul suggests how to approach the discovery of different gifts.

> *For by the grace given to me I say to everyone among you not to think of yourself more highly than you ought to think, but to think with sober judgment, each according to the measure of faith that God has assigned.*
>
> Romans 12:3

The gifts God has created into our very being are clues for ways to live out our calling. Spiritual gifts include both natural abilities and personality traits raised to new heights in Christ's service and fresh outpourings from God for new tasks. Gifts of grace and gifts of the Spirit are given for the purpose of building up the church. The reflection section that follows suggests a procedure to help you begin to discern gifts God may be calling forth in you. While no one is given all the gifts, each one has some gift for God's glory.

> *Like good stewards of the manifold grace of God, serve one another with whatever gift each of you has received. Whoever speaks must do so as one speaking the very words of God; whoever serves must do so with the strength that God supplies, so that God may be glorified in all things through Jesus Christ. To him belong the glory and the power forever and ever. Amen.*
>
> 1 Peter 4:10-11

## RESPOND TO GOD'S CALL IN FAITH AND OBEDIENCE

There is no timetable for discerning God's will for your life, and there are no shortcuts. At some point, however, you will need to step into God's future, acting in confidence that the God who calls also provides the necessary gifts for the task. You will have traveled a long process of discernment with others in the Christian community, and the journey will continue your entire life. You may not fully perceive God's hand in this process until you look back much later, as through a rearview mirror.

## FOR REFLECTION

What gifts do you have for what ministry? The question is best answered in a prayerful relationship with a pastor or another person. One way to begin is by reflecting together on your life.

- Begin to develop an autobiography. Start by jotting down key events, people, and experiences that have shaped who you are. Focus on times you were particularly aware of the presence of God in ordinary, painful, and joyous moments. For some, God is perceived personally and experientially; for others, intellectually and rationally.

- Write summaries of accomplishments that filled you with a sense of joy, achievement, or growth, even if no one noticed what you did. Include activities at school, church, work, and in the community. Add highlights from your leisure time and personal relationships. Identify what you did in each activity.

- Include summaries of any difficult times in your life: times of defeat or failure, discouragement or loss. Include moments of grace as well as times when you experienced the absence of God or testing of faith.

- With another person, look for patterns and trends of abilities that emerge in many of the different activities. Some will be skills you have learned to help you reach your goals. Others may be gifts, those talents and qualities that you exercise quite naturally. Gifts, like skills, require practice and cultivation. They normally bring a deeper level of joy than do skills. Gifts are given for the common good and for God's glory. List the abilities and traits you think may be gifts from God to you.

- Once you have identified possible gifts that are central in your life over time and circumstances, you will be better prepared to discern the settings to which God may be calling you. Now consider the varieties of service described in Chapter 2. Make note of needs in the church and in the world that seem to draw you in.

As you carefully consider the gifts you may have been given, observe how these compare with ministries the church needs. To what extent do you seem to have potential, with appropriate training, to serve as an ordained minister, a diaconal minister, a deaconess, or an associate in ministry? If your gifts appear to be in other areas, in what occupations might your gifts be employed more effectively? To assist you in considering how best to use your abilities and gifts, you may want to utilize the services of a church-related career counseling agency that your synod candidacy committee may recommend.

*Alleluia. Lord, to whom shall we go?*
*You have the words of eternal life. Alleluia.*

*Lutheran Book of Worship*, Holy Communion

# CHAPTER 5

# *What to Expect*

*I*f you are using *What Shall I Say?* to engage in the
process of discernment about God's call for your future,
and especially if you are seeking clarity about whether
you may be called to prepare for ordained or rostered lay
ministry in the church, then you deserve information about
what to expect if you should decide to seek such preparation. This chapter will inform you about the candidacy
process of the Evangelical Lutheran Church in America,
about education and formation for ordained and rostered
lay ministries in the Evangelical Lutheran Church in
America, about the varieties of costs involved in such education, and about formal assignment and call procedures
when you have finished your education.

## THE CANDIDACY PROCESS

Candidacy in the Evangelical Lutheran Church in America
is the churchwide process of preparation and formation
leading to the ordained ministry of Word and Sacrament or
to service as an associate in ministry, ELCA deaconess, or
diaconal minister. Candidacy involves the partnership of
candidate, congregation, candidacy committee, ELCA seminary, and the Division for Ministry of the Evangelical
Lutheran Church in America.

An early concern of candidacy is that of readiness and
discernment. As individuals present themselves to candidacy committees, certain questions must be addressed: Is
there familiarity with Lutheran congregational life? Is there
an understanding of ministry in the life of this church? Is
there a realistic assessment of an individual's potential for
service? Is there a mature faith and commitment to Christ?

Your use of this discernment resource is a part of the first step in candidacy, that of *entrance.* Your synod candidacy committee will provide a setting (retreat or other) in which to reflect on your use of this resource. They may also suggest a mentor to work with you in this time of discernment. You begin the candidacy process by completing the "Application for Candidacy in the ELCA" and by having your congregation register you. You will then be asked to participate in an initial interview with a member of the candidacy committee and receive a psychological and career evaluation by a psychologist approved by the Division for Ministry. Your synod candidacy committee will review the results of these interviews and evaluations and meet with you concerning your readiness to begin theological study. A positive entrance decision enables you to begin study at an ELCA seminary (or other accredited theological school) in preparation for rostered ministry in this church.

During your course of studies (typically at the beginning of the second year of study) you will be considered for *endorsement.* This is a decision that determines your potential as a candidate for a particular form of rostered ministry as a pastor, associate in ministry, diaconal minister, or deaconess. A positive endorsement decision permits a candidate to participate in an ELCA internship or supervised field experience.

The final step in candidacy is that of *approval.* During your final year of study you will be asked to prepare the ELCA Approval Essay, which asks you to give evidence of the integration of your theological studies with the experience gained during your internship and field experience in an ELCA congregation. The candidacy committee that has worked with you during your time of preparation now interviews you and makes a decision concerning your readiness to serve in one of the rostered ministries of the Evangelical Lutheran Church in America. It is a decision that expresses the church's discernment of your gifts and abilities for ministry. As an approved candidate you then participate in the churchwide assignment process and are assigned to a synod where you are available for a letter of call from a congregation or related ministry of that synod. A letter of call is the completion of the journey of discernment; it is an expression of confidence from a congregation of the baptized that you are a leader needed by them in their faith and life. It is a new beginning of service and ministry in your life as a leader of the people of God.

## EDUCATION FOR ORDAINED AND ROSTERED LAY MINISTRIES

The church has always valued education for its leaders. St. Paul exhibits in his writings his thorough training in both Jewish rabbinic studies and Greek philosophical studies. It is no accident that he writes:

> *Finally, beloved, whatever is true, whatever is honorable, whatever is just, whatever is pure, whatever is pleasing, whatever is commendable, if there is any excellence and if there is anything worthy of praise, think about these things.*

> Philippians 4:8-9

True, he came to "regard everything as loss because of the surpassing value of knowing Christ Jesus" (Philippians 3:8). But a sound education serves, rather than replaces, "the surpassing value of knowing Christ."

The Lutheran churches have been especially committed to an educated ministry. Martin Luther was concerned that pastors know Hebrew and Greek, the languages of the Old and New Testaments, and Latin, the learned language of his day. Johann Sebastian Bach (1685–1750), the great Lutheran cantor of St. Thomas church in Leipzig, Germany, received little formal education. But he owned a good theological library, including a well-read and annotated edition of Luther's works. And he went to great lengths to improve his musical skills, including a two-hundred-mile walk to Lubeck, where he stayed for four months in order to learn from the celebrated Dietrich Buxtehude (1637–1707).

All candidates preparing for rostered ministry in the Evangelical Lutheran Church in America are expected to be firmly grounded in knowledge of the Scriptures and the Lutheran doctrinal tradition, and to adhere to the confession of faith of this church. The course of study, preparation, and formation varies according to the needs and demands of the particular form of ministry.

## SEMINARIES OF THE ELCA

Students preparing for ordained and rostered lay ministries in the Evangelical Lutheran Church in America are able to study at North American seminaries and graduate schools of theology that are accredited by the Association of Theological Schools (ATS). However, candidates who seek to serve in the ordained ministry of the Evangelical Lutheran Church in America will be expected to spend the equivalent of at least one full year of study at a seminary of the Evangelical Lutheran Church in America.

Normally, only students with a bachelor's degree from an accredited college or university are admitted to seminary. You should assess your ability to fulfill this academic requirement for admission. Equally important, you might want to ask how your previous education has equipped you for the special demands of seminary study. College studies in the humanities—literature, history, and philosophy—will be of most help in dealing with the texts and logic of theology. College studies in the social sciences—psychology, education, political science, and sociology—will be of most help in preparing for pastoral care and community leadership, as well as diaconal service. College studies in vocations such as business, engineering, and health care, or in technology and the natural sciences, may be of most help in identifying with the many church members who work in such fields.

The Evangelical Lutheran Church in America provides a system of theological education, preparing leaders for church and society. The eight seminaries of the ELCA provide high quality theological education within a Lutheran context. They are: Luther Seminary, St. Paul, Minnesota; Lutheran School of Theology at Chicago; Lutheran Theological Seminary at Gettysburg; The Lutheran Theological Seminary at Philadelphia; Lutheran Theological Southern Seminary, Columbia, South Carolina; Pacific Lutheran Theological Seminary, Berkeley, California; Trinity Lutheran Seminary, Columbus, Ohio; and Wartburg Theological Seminary, Dubuque, Iowa. When you apply for candidacy you will receive a booklet, "Seminaries of the Evangelical Lutheran Church in America," which describes each of these seminaries.

The curricula at the seminaries differ in detail, but at each of the ELCA seminaries you will study the Scriptures of Israel (Old Testament) and the Scriptures of the church (New Testament), the history of the Christian church, systematic theology, ethics, and the mission of the church. Disciplines required for the practice of ministry will vary with the form of service but include such things as preaching and leadership of worship, teaching, counseling, and pastoral care.

In the study of the Scriptures of Israel you will venture into the depths of God's strange and wonderful and desperately painful history with the Jews, from Abraham and Sarah to Anne Frank and Elie Wiesel, from Jacob and Rahab through Ruth and David to the contemporary state of Israel. You will want to rejoice with Paul that God has grafted us gentiles, like "wild olive shoots" onto the "rich root of the olive tree," so that God "may be merciful to all," to Palestinians and Polynesians, to Arabs and Africans, to Slavs and Scandinavians, to Asians and Americans (Romans 11:17-36).

In your study of the Scriptures of the church you will want to drink forever from the fountain of the resurrection of Jesus. You will be living in the last chapter of the world's history, with the Holy Spirit as the down payment on God's future so that you can live in anticipation of the coming reign of God as if it were already here. You will discover from the gospel that you are free to invest yourself in our current chapter of the world's history with joyful abandon, that however much or however little God lets you do, you will participate in Christ's changing the course of the world's history!

Throughout your study you will grow in faith and knowledge as you retrieve the past from the wonderful vantage point of Jesus' resurrection. You will understand the cross of Jesus as something that has happened to the Father and the Son in the Holy Spirit, the ultimate vulnerability of suffering Love willing and able to endure the agony of alienation so that now nothing, "neither death, nor life, nor angels, nor rulers, nor things present, nor things to come, nor powers, nor height, nor depth, nor anything else in all creation, will be able to separate us from the love of God in Christ Jesus our Lord" (Romans 8:38-39).

Because of the resurrection of Jesus you will want to pay attention to all of Jesus' history available to us in the Gospels, with the insight of the Holy Spirit giving you one "aha!" after another, hearing yourself say again and again, "So that's what this story means!"

The resurrection of Jesus will let you retrieve your own past, so that you can remember with truth, not self-deception; so that you can accept yourself with thanksgiving, not despair; so that you can confess what is necessary to confess, not hide behind the fig leaf of blaming others; so that you can receive God's justification of your life with faith, not strive to justify your life with your own accomplishments.

The resurrection of Jesus will free you to encounter the historical church, warts and all. Despite its evident faults the church will nevertheless "abide forever," (Augsburg Confession, Article VII). You will discover God's gifts of institutional structure for the church, the gifts of eucharistic liturgy and faithful preaching, the faithful response of the church's mission and witness, and the gifts of ministry by the whole people of God. You will learn about the gifts of ministry exercised by pastors and bishops, diaconal ministers and deaconesses, and associates in ministry, who serve as administrators, theologians and chaplains, teachers, and musicians.

You will receive the gifts of Holy Scripture, together with its commentaries and dictionaries, encyclopedias and word studies, interpreters and their arguments. You will receive the gifts of creeds and confessions; the history of dogmatic battles over the truth of the gospel; the examples of confessors like Perpetua and Felicity, martyrs at Carthage in A.D. 203, and Simon Schneeweiss (his name is "snow white" in German), once pastor at Crailsheim, Germany, and signer of the Smalcald Articles in A.D.1537.

## Preparing to Be an Ordained Minister

Your course of study leading to the ordained ministry of Word and Sacrament will include three years of academic work and one year of internship in a congregation of the Evangelical Lutheran Church in America. You will also fulfill a requirement, usually one academic quarter, in supervised clinical ministry (normally a unit of clinical pastoral education).

## Preparing to Be an Associate in Ministry

Your course of study will include a bachelor's degree in a field appropriate to the area of specialization: education, music and the arts, administration, or service. Additionally, associates in ministry must receive twenty semester credits in theological studies. The theological education requirement may be met either at the undergraduate or graduate level or through a specifically approved course of study such as SELECT or other extension curricula. Associates in ministry complete a unit of supervised field experience as well.

## Preparing to Be a Diaconal Minister

Your course of study includes a master's degree in theological study from an accredited school in North America (normally two years), including Lutheran theological study, completion of the formational component for diaconal ministry, and completion of an approved internship. Diaconal ministers are required to demonstrate competence as well in at least one area of specialization, or to hold professional credentials in an appropriate field related to diaconal ministry. The ELCA has a center for the preparation of diaconal ministers that provides curriculum, program design, contextual education, and formation designed to meet the particular needs of diaconal ministers. Candidates for diaconal ministers study with candidates for ordained ministry, sharing many of the same basic theological education courses, while at the same time developing their diaconal identity and focus for mission.

## Preparing to Be an ELCA Deaconess
Your course of study includes completion of the educational requirements as established by the Deaconess Community of the Evangelical Lutheran Church in America. All deaconess candidates receive graduate-level theological education, with most required to complete a first professional theological degree. Deaconess candidates all participate in the formation process of the Deaconess Community.

## Admission to an ELCA Seminary
Each ELCA seminary is prepared to help you evaluate your readiness for admission. Each seminary will explain in as much detail as you request what is required for its various degree programs and how these requirements will prepare you for ordination or rostered ministry. A visit to one or more seminaries will be of great value in helping you decide which seminary will be most suitable for you.

## The Costs of Seminary Education
No student ever pays the full financial cost of education. Support from the Evangelical Lutheran Church in America and from each seminary's endowment fund will pay for 60 percent or more of your education. It will be necessary for you to learn from each seminary what your direct costs are. Then you must ask what percentage of those costs can be paid by scholarships and grants. Perhaps your own home congregation will also be able to pay some of your costs. The seminaries can assist you in applying for and obtaining deferred interest loans to pay for your educational costs.

However, you will want to pay for as little of your education with loans as possible. Salaries for ordained and rostered lay ministers vary, but most of them offer little opportunity for making large payments on educational loans. This becomes a special problem if you are already bringing with you to seminary education significant indebtedness from your undergraduate education.

When you have gathered as much information as you need about your costs, your debts, and your resources, it will be helpful and important for you to discuss your situation with a trusted financial advisor. If you have discerned that you have a genuine call to ordained or rostered ministry, and if you have received encouragement from the church in the process of discernment, then a way will surely be found to acquire the education you need.

Money is only one of the costs. Time is the other significant cost. Theological education is challenging and takes time for reading and reflection, for attending classes and fulfilling assignments, for participating in congregational life and acquiring the skills of ministry. If you are married and if you have growing children then you have prior and very important vocations involving your spouse and your children that you must not neglect. You will want to make out a "time budget" as well as a financial budget. You will want to involve your spouse appropriately in what you are learning so that together you can share the changes that are taking place in you as a result of your theological education.

The important point is that there is limited time available for gainful employment while you are student. You must count on setting priorities for your expenditure of money and time if you are to respond appropriately to your call.

## ASSIGNMENT AND CALL

As an approved candidate for rostered ministry in the Evangelical Lutheran Church in America you will participate in the churchwide assignment process. The ELCA expects that most, if not all, of its candidates for rostered ministry are ready and available for assignment to any region of the church, ready and available for ministry in congregations of any synod of the church. You will, of course, be able to identify preferences in terms of region and synod. However, the mission and ministry needs of the church must be a priority in the assignment of candidates.

If there are valid reasons, such as considerations that involve health or the employment or education of a spouse, that limit you to a specific geographical region, such limitations can be taken into account. But such limitations will probably mean that it will be difficult for you to be recommended for call to a congregation. This is especially the case if the place to which you are limited is the location of the seminary where you are studying.

This information is meant to assist you in the process of discernment. It is possible that the information confronts you with difficulties or apparent obstacles as you seek to discern whether you are called to ordained or rostered lay ministry in the Evangelical Lutheran Church in America. But you deserve straight talk, full and appropriate information, if you are to engage in an authentic process of discernment. Discerning God's will means taking into account as many factors as can reasonably be considered. It means facing and dealing with difficulties and apparent obstacles, not ignoring or avoiding them. Courage for facing challenges is also God's gift.

*Almighty God, you gave your Son both as a sacrifice for sin and a model of the godly life. Enable us to receive him always with thanksgiving, and to conform our lives to his; through the same Jesus Christ our Lord. Amen.*

*Lutheran Book of Worship*, Holy Communion

You shall receive power when the Holy Spirit
has come upon you; and you shall be my
witnesses in Jerusalem and in all Judea and
Samaria and to the end of the earth.

Acts 1:8

# CHAPTER 6

# *Power for*
# *the Challenge*

*W*e have tried to give you straight talk, information, and introduction to factors appropriate for
discernment of God's call. If you have read this
far, you yourself will be able to judge whether or not we
have succeeded. Now for some concluding words, some
words we hope are encouraging ones.

In straight talk there is both good news and bad news.
According to the first chapter, the good news could hardly
be better. It is the triune God's own good news: Jesus is the
risen Messiah! "Death no longer has dominion over him"
(Romans 6:9). Life, not death, will have the last word—for
each of us, and for the whole cosmos. The reign of God,
with its hope and promise, will triumph. We have the great
good fortune to have been grasped by this astonishing good
news in our baptism. We are called to be its witnesses!

The "bad" news is that "servants are not greater than
their master" (John 15:20). So there it is. The vision that
calls us plunges us into struggle within ourselves. That is
what makes our baptism an awesome reality. The struggle
will be between the urgent desire to protect ourselves at all
costs and the incredible freedom to offer ourselves into the
service of the triune God.

The vision that calls us also plunges us into the further
struggle between our witness to the gospel and the indiffer-
ence or even hostility that we will and do encounter. Still
worse will be the temptation to distort or pervert the
church, to betray the vision by making the church into
something it is not called to be. Worst of all will be the
temptations not to want to know that we are doing this.

The challenge inherent in the call to be witnesses of Jesus' resurrection is daunting. Perhaps that is why Frederick Buechner tells the story of the evening at dinner when he announced to his family his intention to enroll in seminary. Conversation stopped. His dowager aunt, presiding at the meal as she did over the family, glared at him for an uncomfortably long time. Then she broke the silence: "Did you decide this on your own, or were you badly advised?"

Good question. Especially, "were you badly advised?" She didn't just think that Buechner had made a mistake when comparing his abilities with those needed for a vocation to ordained Christian ministry. She thought that the whole enterprise of ordained ministry in the church was a mistake!

Obviously we don't agree with her, and not only because we want you to give serious consideration to the possibility that God may be calling you to ordained or rostered lay ministry in the Evangelical Lutheran Church in America. We don't agree because we believe that there is power for the challenge, and resources available for those who are called.

Nineteenth-century Bishop Phillips Brooks, in one of his greatest sermons, lifted up the authentic relationship between challenge and power. "Do not pray for easy lives," he said. "Pray to be stronger [persons]! Do not pray for tasks equal to your powers. Pray for powers equal to your tasks!"

Those "powers equal to tasks" were available to Abraham and Sarah; to Moses and Miriam; to Ruth and Esther; to Isaiah and Jeremiah; to Mary and Joseph; to Phoebe and Paul; to Augustine's pious mother Monica; to Macrina, sister and teacher to some of the great Greek theologians of the fourth century A.D.; to bishop and confessor

Athanasius of Alexandria; to Thomas Aquinas, the greatest of medieval theologians.

They were available to Catherine of Siena and Birgitta of Sweden; to Bartolomé de Las Casas, the courageous champion of Indian rights in Mexico four hundred years ago; to German martyrs Dietrich Bonhoeffer and Helmuth von Moltke in this century; to reformers Martin Luther and Pope John XXIII; to Japanese theologian Kazoh Kitamori, who recovered the Jewish confession of the suffering God; and to African-American martyr Martin Luther King Jr., who gave eloquent expression to God's dream for all people. Those powers continue to be available to countless Christian people today—and to you.

For more encouragement listen to the words of Pastor Paul Adams, who graduated from a Lutheran seminary in 1922, and who, at age 97, was still remembering and telling stories of his more than seventy years of ordained ministry. When he finished, he looked at a group of seminary students and, with a twinkling in his eyes, he said, "If I had my life to live over again, I would." Other stories like this one could be told by church musicians, day school teachers, deaconesses, chaplains, and others who serve the church in rostered ministry.

The challenge is great, and the need is urgent. But the gospel is greater than every challenge, and the vision of the reign of God for the world is more urgent than any need. Jesus did not want his disciples to ignore the challenge. He said:

> *For which of you, intending to build a tower, does not first sit down and estimate the cost, to see whether he has enough to complete it? Otherwise, when he has laid a foundation and is not able to finish, all who see it will begin to ridicule him, saying, "this fellow began to build*

> *and was not able to finish." Or what king, going out to*
> *wage war against another king, will not sit down first and*
> *consider whether he is able with ten thousand to oppose*
> *the one who comes against him with twenty thousand? If*
> *he cannot, then, while the other is still far away, he sends*
> *a delegation and asks for the terms of peace.*
>
> Luke 14:28-32

He also told his disciples that if they sought to preserve their lives, they would lose them anyway. But "those who lose their life for my sake, and for the sake of the gospel, will save it" (Mark 8:35).

It is clear that Jesus is not talking about careers or jobs, where one is concerned about long-range prospects and fringe benefits. Jesus is talking about something very different. Something grand, something all-encompassing, something necessary, vital, urgent, life-giving, eternal. He told two short parables about that which could grasp us utterly, unconditionally:

> *The kingdom of heaven is like treasure hidden in a field,*
> *which someone found and hid; then in his joy he goes and*
> *sells all that he has and buys that field.*
> *Again, the kingdom of heaven is like a merchant in*
> *search of fine pearls; on finding one pearl of great value,*
> *he went and sold all that he had and bought it.*
>
> Matthew 13:44-45

Consider this. Because Jesus is risen from the dead, everything is changed. History no longer has a depressingly predictable outcome. The world is no longer destined for Stephen Hawking's "big crunch." Your hopes, the hopes of every human being, are determined by Jesus, the Christ, the final judge. "For as all die in Adam, so all will be made alive in Christ." He will put all enemies under his feet, and "the last enemy to be destroyed is death" (1 Corinthians 15:22-27).

That is why the church is called to be different than every other human community. That is why ordained and rostered lay ministries in the church have the power to call the church to its authentic witness.

To be in on the reign of God is to be in on the single most important thing in time and in eternity, to be in on something so important that everything else pales into insignificance. To sell all for such a "pearl" and such a treasured field is neither sacrificial nor heroic. Those in Jesus' short parables behave like persons who have made a great discovery and have had extraordinary luck in doing so. They experienced a profound freedom "known only to those captivated by truly important things."[7]

There is urgency, but do not be overwhelmed by it. Take the time you need. Discern and discover. The triune God is calling you to discern your place in the great ministry of witness to the reign of God, the great ministry of witness to the resurrection of Jesus. If you have heard the gospel, received the call, accepted Jesus' sending of you in your baptism, then, in the end, you will either continue to live out your baptism through your ministry in the world, or you will become part of the ordained or rostered lay ministries of the church. All are the calling of the triune God. One or the other is for you.

*Holy God, mighty Lord, gracious Father: Endless is your mercy and eternal your reign.*

*You have filled all creation with light and life; heaven and earth are full of your glory.*

*Through Abraham you promised to bless all nations. You rescued Israel, your chosen people.*

*Through the prophets you renewed your promise; and, at this end of all the ages, you sent your Son, who in words and deeds proclaimed your kingdom and was obedient to your will, even to giving his life. . . .*

*Therefore, gracious Father, with this bread and cup we remember the life our Lord offered for us.*

*And, believing the witness of his resurrection, we await his coming in power to share with us the great and promised feast.*

*Lutheran Book of Worship*, Holy Communion

# Notes

1. Robert Jenson, *A Large Catechism* (New York: American Lutheran Publicity Bureau, 1991), 28–29.

2. Martin Luther, *The Large Catechism*, in *The Book of Concord*, trans. and ed. Theodore G. Tappert (Philadelphia: Muhlenburg Press, 1959), 417.

3. Martin Luther, "Sermon on Day of St. John the Evangelist: Everyone Should Honor His Calling and Be Content in It," *Church Postils*, in *The Precious and Sacred Writings of Martin Luther* vol. 10, ed. John. N. Lenker (Minneapolis: Lutherans of All Lands Co., 1905), 242–243.

4. Frederick Buechner, *Wishful Thinking. A Theological ABC* (New York: Harper and Row, 1973), 95.

5. Tappert, 31.

6. Quoted by Marilyn Stulken, *Hymnal Companion to the Lutheran Book of Worship* (Philadelphia: Fortress Press, 1981), 333.

7. Gerhard Lohfink, *Jesus and Community* (Philadelphia: Fortress Press, 1984), 60–61.

## Selected Bibliography

Arias, Chris. *Discernment: Seeking God in Every Situation.* Hauppauge, N.Y.: Living Flame Press, 1981, 1988.

Arias, Mortimer. *Announcing the Reign of God.* Philadelphia: Fortress Press, 1984. (Out of print.)

Bolles, Richard. *How to Find Your Mission in Life.* Berkeley, Calif.: Ten Speed Press, 1991.

Bonhoeffer, Dietrich. *Life Together.* San Francisco: Harper and Row, 1976.

Buechner, Frederick. *The Sacred Journey.* San Francisco: Harper and Row, 1982.

Farnham, Suzanne G., Joseph P. Gill, R. Taylor McLean, and Susan M. Ward. *Listening Hearts: Discerning Call in Community.* Harrisburg, Pa.: Moorhouse Publishing, 1997.

Fischer, Kathleen. *Feminist Perspectives on Spiritual Direction.* New York: Paulist Press, 1988.

Heiges, Donald R. *The Christian's Calling.* Philadelphia: Fortress Press, 1984 revised ed. (Out of print.)

Jenson, Robert. *A Large Catechism.* Delhi, New York: The American Lutheran Publicity Bureau, 1991.

Kelsey, Morton T. *Adventure Inward: Christian Growth through Person Journal Writing.* Minneapolis: Augsburg, 1980.

Lewis, Roy. *Choosing Your Career, Finding Your Vocation: A Step-by-Step Guide for Adults and Counselors.* Mahwah, N.J.: Paulist Press, 1989.

Lohfink, Gerhard. *Jesus and Community*. Philadelphia: Fortress Press, 1984.

Mead, Loren B. *The Once and Future Church: Reinventing the Congregation for a New Mission Frontier*. Washington, D.C.: The Alban Institute, Inc., 1991.

Nichol, Todd, and Marc Kolden, ed. *Called and Ordained: Lutheran Perspectives on the Office of the Ministry*. Minneapolis: Fortress Press, 1990. (Out of print.)

Nouwen, Henri J. M. *Reaching Out: The Three Movements of the Spiritual Life*. Garden City, N.Y.: Doubleday and Co., 1986.

## ADDITIONAL RESOURCES

These resources may be ordered from the ELCA Distribution Center, 1-800-328-4648.

*Vision and Expectations—Ordained Ministers in the Evangelical Lutheran Church in America.* 69-009440

*How About You?* A 10-minute video portraying ministry in the Evangelical Lutheran Church in America. 69-004926